The Three Billy Goats Gruff

WRITTEN BY
VIVIAN FRENCH
ILLUSTRATED BY
ARTHUR ROBINS

WALKER BOOKS
AND SUBSIDIARIES
LONDON • BOSTON • SYDNEY

First published 2000 by Walker Books Ltd
87 Vauxhall Walk, London SE11 5HJ

4 6 8 10 9 7 5 3

Text © 2000 Vivian French
Illustrations © 2000 Arthur Robins

This book has been typeset in Bold Sassoon Primary.

Printed in Singapore

British Library Cataloguing in Publication Data
A catalogue record for this book is
available from the British Library.

ISBN 0-7445-6852-8

Notes for Children

The Three Billy Goats Gruff is the story of three clever goats who trick a great big scary troll.
You may know the story already, but it doesn't matter if you don't.

This book is a little different from other picture books. You will be sharing it with other people and telling the story together.

You can read

this line

this line

this line

or this line.

Even when someone else is reading, try to follow the words. It will help when it's your turn!

Once upon a time—

I know that beginning!

That's how stories always begin.

That's right.

Once upon a time there were three—

Three little pigs!

No. Not three little pigs.

Three bears in a wood!

No. Not three bears in a wood.

What was it then?

Three billy goats.

I know this one!

So do I!

Once upon a time

There were three billy goats,

Three billy goats called Gruff.

They lived in a field

And they ate all the grass.

There was no grass left.

No grass at all.

But over the bridge

The ricketty racketty bridge

There was another field –

A green green field

By the blue blue stream.

"Let's go over the bridge

The ricketty racketty bridge,"

Said Little Billy Goat Gruff.

"We can eat grass all day,"

Said Middle-sized Billy Goat Gruff.

"All day and every day,"

Said Great Big Billy Goat Gruff.

Little Billy Goat Gruff went first.

He went over the bridge.

No he didn't!

Yes he did.

No he didn't! What about the troll?

The what?

The troll.

You can't forget about the troll!

What did the troll do?

Wait and see!

Little Billy Goat Gruff came to the bridge

And he began to skip across –

Tip! Tap! Tip! Tap!

Over the ricketty racketty bridge.

When all of a sudden—

Quick! Turn the page!

UP! jumped the troll.

The great big troll.

The great big hairy troll.

The great big hairy scary troll.

And he said,

"WHO'S THAT TIPPING AND TAPPING

OVER MY RICKETTY RACKETTY BRIDGE?"

Little Billy Goat Gruff said, "Me!"

"WHO ARE YOU?"

roared the troll.

"I'm Little Billy Goat Gruff

And I'm skipping over the bridge

The ricketty racketty bridge."

"OH NO YOU'RE NOT!" roared the troll.

"LITTLE BILLY GOAT GRUFF,

I'M GOING TO EAT YOU FOR MY DINNER!"

What did Little Billy Goat Gruff do?

What did Little Billy Goat Gruff say?

He said, "Please don't eat me, Mr Troll.

I'm much too little to be your dinner."

"BUT I'M HUNGRY!" roared the troll.

"Wait," said Little Billy Goat Gruff.

"Middle-sized Billy Goat Gruff is coming

And he's much bigger than me!"

"Very well, then," said the troll.

"Be on your way."

So Little Billy Goat Gruff

Skipped over the bridge –

Tip! Tap! Tip! Tap!

And he ate the grass in the field,

The green green field,

All day.

What did the troll do?

The hairy scary troll?

He went back under the bridge.

He went under the bridge to hide.

He went under the bridge to wait.

He was waiting for his dinner.

He was hungry.

"I WANT MY DINNER!"

Then along came the next billy goat,

Middle-sized Billy Goat Gruff –

Trip! Trap! Trip! Trap!

Over the ricketty racketty bridge.

Oooooh!

What's the matter?

I know what's going to happen next!

Quick! Turn the page!

UP! jumped the troll.

The great big troll.

The great big hairy troll.

The great big hairy scary troll.

And he said,

"WHO'S THAT TRIPPING AND TRAPPING

OVER MY RICKETTY RACKETTY BRIDGE?"

Middle-sized Billy Goat Gruff said, "Me!"

"AND WHO ARE YOU?"

roared the troll.

"I'm Middle-sized Billy Goat Gruff

And I'm walking over the bridge

The ricketty racketty bridge."

"OH NO YOU'RE NOT!" roared the troll.

"MIDDLE-SIZED BILLY GOAT GRUFF,

I'M GOING TO EAT YOU FOR MY DINNER!"

What did Middle-sized Billy Goat Gruff do?

What did Middle-sized Billy Goat Gruff say?

He said, "Please don't eat me, Mr Troll.

I'm much too little to be your dinner."

"BUT I'M HUNGRY!" roared the troll.

"Wait," said Middle-sized Billy Goat Gruff.

"Great Big Billy Goat Gruff is coming

And he's much bigger than me!"

"Very well, then," said the troll.

"Be on your way."

So Middle-sized Billy Goat Gruff

Walked over the bridge –

Trip! Trap! Trip! Trap!

And he ate the grass in the field,

The green green field,

All day.

I know what the troll did!

The hairy scary troll.

He went back under the bridge.

He went under the bridge to hide.

He went under the bridge to wait.

He was waiting for his dinner.

He was hungry.

He was very hungry!

Then along came the next billy goat,

Great Big Billy Goat Gruff –

Stamp! Stamp! Stamp! Stamp!

Over the ricketty racketty bridge.

The bridge shook and rattled –

Rattle! Rattle! Rattle!

And then,

All of a sudden—

UP! jumped the troll.

The great big troll.

The great big hairy troll.

The great big hairy scary troll.

And he said,

"WHO'S THAT STAMPING AND STAMPING

OVER MY RICKETTY RACKETTY BRIDGE?"

Great Big Billy Goat Gruff said, "Me!"

"AND WHO ARE YOU?"

roared the troll.

"I'm Great Big Billy Goat Gruff

And I'm stamping over the bridge

The ricketty racketty bridge."

"OH NO YOU'RE NOT!" roared the troll.

"GREAT BIG BILLY GOAT GRUFF,

I'M GOING TO EAT YOU FOR MY DINNER!"

But Great Big Billy Goat Gruff said,

"Oh no you're not!"

And the troll said,

"OH YES I AM!"

And Great Big Billy Goat Gruff said,

"Oh no you're not!"

And the troll said,

"OH YES I AM!"

And Great Big Billy Goat Gruff said,

"OH NO YOU'RE NOT!"

And he rushed at the troll

And he dashed at the troll –

STAMPETTY! STAMPETTY! STAMPETTY!

And then—

Quick! Quick!

Turn the page!

Great Big Billy Goat Gruff

Tossed the troll

Over the bridge

And into the stream

With a great big

SPLASH!

Then Great Big Billy Goat Gruff

And Middle-sized Billy Goat Gruff

And Little Billy Goat Gruff

Lived happily ever after

In the green green field

By the blue blue stream.

Notes for Teachers

Story Plays are written and presented in a way that encourages children to read aloud together. They are dramatic versions of memorable and exciting stories, told in strongly patterned language which gives children the chance to practise at a vital stage of their reading development. Sharing stories in this way makes reading an active and enjoyable process, and one that draws in even the reticent reader.

The story is told by four different voices, divided into four colours so that each child can easily read his or her part. The blue line is for more experienced readers; the red line for less experienced readers. When there are more than four children in a group, there is an ideal opportunity for paired reading. Partnering a more experienced reader with a less experienced one can be very supportive and provides a learning experience for both children.

Story Plays encourage children to share in the reading of a whole text in a collaborative and interactive way. This makes them perfect for group and guided reading activities. Children will find they need to pay close attention to the print and punctuation, and to use the meaning of the whole story in order to read it with expression and a real sense of voice.

The Big Book version can be used to introduce children to *Story Plays* in shared reading sessions. The class can be divided into groups to take part in reading the text aloud together, creating a lively performance.